The Causes of World War II

Paul Dowswell

Heinemann Library
Chicago, Illinois

© 2003 Heinemann Library
a division of Reed Elsevier Inc.
Chicago, Illinois

Customer Service 888-454-2279

Visit our website at www.heinemannlibrary.com

Produced for Heinemann Library by Discovery Books
Designed by Ian Winton
Consultant: Stewart Ross
Picture research by Rachel Tisdale
Originated by Dot Gradations
Printed in China

07 06 05 04
10 9 8 7 6 5 4 3 2

Library of Congress Cataloging-in-Publication Data
Dowswell, Paul.
  The causes of World War II / Paul Dowswell.
      p. cm. -- (20th-century perspectives)
Summary: Examines the causes of World War II, including the stipulations of the treaty that Germany was forced to sign at the end of World War I, the effects of the Great Depression, Germany's desire for colonies, and the rise of Hitler.
Includes bibliographical references and index.
  ISBN 1-40340-149-7 (HC), 1-4034-4621-0 (Pbk.)
  1. World War, 1939-1945--Causes--Juvenile literature. 2. Germany--Politics and government--1918-1933--Juvenile literature. 3. Germany--Politics and government--1933-1945--Juvenile literature. 4. National socialism--Juvenile literature. [1. World War, 1939-1945--Causes. 2. Germany--Politics and government--1918-1933. 3. Germany--Politics and government--1933-1945. 4. National socialism.] I. Title: Causes of World War Two. II. Title: Causes of World War 2. III. Title. IV. Series.
  D741 .D69 2002
  940.53'11--dc21
                          2002004696

Acknowledgments
The author and publishers are grateful to the following for permission to reproduce copyright material: pp. 4, 12, 33, 42 Hulton Deutsch; pp. 5, 7 Peter Newark; pp. 6, 13, 16, 21, 28, 29, 35 Hulton Getty; pp. 8, 15, 17, 20, 23 Mary Evans Picture Library; pp. 10, 14 Peter Newark's American Pictures; pp. 11, 18, 27, 32 Corbis; pp. 19, 38, 43 Peter Newark's Military Pictures; pp. 22, 25, 26, 30, 34, 37, 40 Hulton Archive; pp. 24, 36 David King Collection.

Cover photograph reproduced with permission of Hulton Archive. Adolf Hitler is shown being welcomed by German-speaking children in the Sudetenland in 1938.

Some words are shown in bold, **like this.** You can find out what they mean by looking in the glossary.

Contents

World War II Begins

For the dozen or so German prisoners held by **Nazi SS** soldiers near the Polish border, the last day of August 1939 was to be the last day of their lives. All had been condemned to death and had passed their final weeks in brutal confinement. Now they were herded out of a prison van and into an army barracks, where they were ordered to take off their prison clothes and put on uniforms of the Polish army. Then, one by one, they were led away. What thoughts passed through their minds in their last bewildered moments we will never know, but their fate was to be truly bizarre. There is little chance that the prisoners were able to guess what would happen next.

Each prisoner was given an injection that made him unconscious. Then all were carried into another van, which was driven to a radio station close to the Polish border. The men were dumped outside the station, and bullets were fired into their bodies. Then, newspaper reporters and press photographers arrived to record the whole grisly scene.

War begins

At dawn the next day, September 1, a German invasion force of about two million men poured into Poland. Adolf Hitler, the Nazi leader, referred to the staged event when he claimed that the invasion was provoked by a Polish attack on a German radio station.

While German bombers attacked the Polish capital of Warsaw and destroyed airfields and fuel dumps behind the front line, German dive-bomber planes, tanks, and artillery destroyed Polish frontline troops. This was the world's introduction to a new form of warfare called *blitzkrieg*. Blitzkrieg used **motorized troops** that followed behind tanks and aircraft, which moved rapidly forward. The Polish army fought bravely, but it was completely outmatched. The Polish army even sent cavalry, or soldiers on horses, into action against German tanks. To make matters worse, the Soviet Union attacked Poland on September 17.

Nazi soldiers march through Poland and into battle in September 1939. World War II had just begun. The conflict was to continue for nearly six years.

As the German army continued to move east, Poland's startled peasants could only watch in numb amazement. The arrogant young soldiers in gray-green uniforms who swept through their towns were frightening enough. But the soldiers who followed were more terrifying. They wore sinister black uniforms with death's head insignias, which were badges or emblems with human skulls on them.

The soldiers dressed in black were members of Heinrich Himmler's SS *Einsatzgruppen,* which were the German commander's special forces. Their task was to kill anyone thought capable of organizing resistance to the Nazis, such as army officers, teachers, or academics. In the years that were to follow, they were also instructed to round up any Jews they could find. Many Jews were killed where they were found, but others were taken to **ghettos** in Warsaw and other cities. Later, they were taken to **concentration camps,** where they were eventually killed. Over the next five and a half years of war, Poland would suffer so badly that almost one in five of its population would be killed.

It took barely a month for Poland to be conquered. Hitler and Nazi Germany were now left in possession of the whole of central Europe. The Nazi leader had hoped to gain Poland without stirring up a general European war, but he had miscalculated badly. Within two days of the invasion, France and Great Britain had both declared war on Germany, so marking the beginning of World War II.

The Nazis wasted no time in victimizing their enemies. These Polish Jews are being put to work in a forced labor camp near Warsaw, less than a month after the German invasion.

Hitler and Poland

"Close your hearts to pity. Act brutally. Whatever we find in the shape of an upper class in Poland is to be **liquidated** . . . [We must] ensure that the Polish **intelligentsia** cannot throw up a new leader class."
Hitler's orders on the eve of the invasion of Poland, August 1939.

What Were the Causes of World War II?

"World War II" is a term used to describe a series of wars that took place in different parts of the world between 1939 and 1945. Some historians think the war began in 1937 when Japan invaded China, while others give 1939 as the year, when Germany invaded Poland. But these different conflicts only developed into a true world war when the United States joined the fighting in 1941. The war in Europe ended in May 1945, and the war in East Asia ended three months later.

Flag-waving Londoners, some civilians, some in military uniforms, celebrate the **armistice** *on November 11, 1918. Little did they realize that the peace was only temporary.*

There are many reasons why World War II started. In this book, we will explain some of the most important ones. To begin with, we need to look at the effects of the Treaty of Versailles, which was signed after World War I. We will also examine the role of the League of Nations, which was also established after World War I. We will consider how the effects of the Great **Depression** helped to bring extreme political **regimes** such as the **Nazis** to power. Some of the attitudes and policies of the **Allied** countries, such as "**appeasement**" and "**isolationism,**" will also be examined. But first, we need to look at events that took place earlier in the 20th century, when World War I was being fought.

World War I

World War I (1914–18) was such a terrible, destructive war that those who fought it tried to convince themselves that all the suffering and sacrifice they endured had been for some greater good. During the conflict, it was often referred to as the "Great War," but in fact, the Great War was only the beginning. Another war less than twenty years later would be much worse. Barely five years after the Great War ended in 1918, it was already being referred to as "The *First* World War."

The causes of World War I were many and complex. Rival **alliances** had been made by opposing European nations that were building up their armed forces in an effort to hold onto or gain more military power. Fierce competition over **colonies** was also a factor. Germany was a powerful, wealthy nation, but it had only a few colonies. France and Great Britain, which were Germany's rivals in Europe, had huge colonial **empires,** mostly in Asia and Africa. These colonies provided **raw materials** and cheap labor, as well as the prestige of being a "world power."

Germany, Austria-Hungary, and their allies fought Britain, France, and their allies in World War I mainly to defend or improve their position in the world. For four years, the war in western Europe had been a bloody **stalemate.** But in eastern Europe, Germany had achieved great success. In early 1918, Germany made peace with its other major enemy, Russia, and gained territory in eastern Europe. With Russia out of the war, Germany turned its full attention to western Europe. But in the summer of 1918, the nation ran out of steam just when fresh American troops were joining the exhausted Allied armies of Britain and France.

A muddled ending

By November 1918, the German army was retreating back to its own western borders. Fearing a **communist revolution** in their war-weary nation similar to the one that had overwhelmed Russia in 1917, Germany's leaders called for peace. But this retreat had been kept from the German people, some of whom still believed their armies were winning the war.

German war graves on the Western Front in November 1918. These graves represent a tiny fraction of the ten million soldiers who were killed in World War I.

The fighting stopped, and complex negotiations began at the Palace of Versailles in France. As a defeated nation, Germany had no say in the discussions that took place or in the final terms of the treaty. The **delegates** at the conference decided, rather unfairly according to some historians, that Germany was responsible for starting the war. German soldiers, and much of German society, were left with a sense of deep betrayal and bitterness at the end of a war they had appeared to be winning at one time. Nothing they fought for had been achieved, and in the years after the war, Germany was to be punished and humiliated.

The Treaty of Versailles

Leaders of the victorious nations of World War I are shown here arriving at peace talks in Versailles. U.S. President Woodrow Wilson (center left) walks alongside French Prime Minister Georges Clemenceau (center).

"We have won the war; now we have to win the peace, and it may be more difficult." So spoke French Prime Minister Georges Clemenceau at the start of the peace conference that was held in the Palace of Versailles in France in the summer of 1919. Although Germany had called for an **armistice** the previous fall, it was on the understanding that it would be treated fairly. But over the winter and spring, the attitudes of some of the victors hardened. They intended to make Germany pay for peace. This resulted in a settlement that no one was happy with.

Making a lasting peace?

The main problem was that the victors were divided on how best to ensure peace in Europe. U.S. President Woodrow Wilson proposed that an international organization for solving conflicts among nations be set up. This organization became known as the League of Nations. He also put forward a set of proposals that, along with other ideas, were known as the

"Fourteen Points." The proposals concerned free trade and disarmament and the right of nations to decide their own futures. Wilson was anxious for **reconciliation** with Germany. However, Great Britain and France, represented by their prime ministers David Lloyd-George and Georges Clemenceau, had other ideas. Clemenceau was determined that Germany should never again be strong enough to threaten France's position in the world, so he wanted a peace treaty that would leave Germany permanently weak. Lloyd-George did not want such harsh measures, but he felt bound to support his wartime **ally** Clemenceau. The fierce hostility that many British politicians and much of the British public felt toward Germany also hindered Lloyd-George's position at the conference.

Verdicts on Versailles

"Those who sign this treaty will sign the death sentence of many millions of German men, women, and children."
Count Ulrich von Brockdorff-Rantzau, head of the German delegation

"We shall have to do the whole thing over again in 25 years at three times the cost."
Lloyd-George, British prime minister

However, the idea of the League of Nations was accepted, and its headquarters was established in Geneva, Switzerland, in 1920. Agreement regarding the fate of Germany was also reached. The main points of the Treaty of Versailles were:

- Germany was to accept responsibility for starting the war.
- Germany was to pay **reparations,** or compensation, to its former enemies totaling $33 billion dollars.
- Germany lost territory to France, Poland, and Belgium. The result of this was that several million Germans now found themselves living in different countries.
- Germany's overseas **colonies** were given to other countries, especially Britain, France, and Japan.
- The German army was to be restricted to 100,000 men.
- No tanks, aircraft, submarines, or heavy artillery were permitted in Germany.

The treaty was signed in June 1919, but it was weakened from the very beginning. Against the wishes of President Wilson, the United States Senate refused to accept the peace treaty. Also, the Senate would not allow the United States to join the League of Nations, which they believed only protected the positions of Britain and France. Wilson, who had already suffered a severe stroke, felt humiliated. With his spirit broken, his health never recovered.

Europe after World War I. As a result of the postwar treaties, thousands of Germans found themselves living outside the newly created borders of Germany.

Other treaties that changed national boundaries

Alongside Germany, three other empires fell during World War I—Austria-Hungary, Russia, and Ottoman Turkey. Treaties were signed that changed Europe's borders and created new countries. Under the Treaty of Brest-Litovsk (March 1918), Russia lost territory to Finland, Latvia, Estonia, Lithuania, and Poland. In the Treaty of St. Germain-en Laye (September 1919), Austria lost territory to Czechoslovakia, Yugoslavia, Poland, Hungary, and Italy. Hungary lost territory to Czechoslovakia, Romania, and Yugoslavia in the Treaty of Trianon (June 1920).

Unfortunately, the redrawing of national boundaries caused more problems than it solved.

Shifting Powers

Today we think of the idea of **colonies**—countries ruled by other countries that take advantage of their **natural resources** and population—as being unfair. But until the middle of the 20th century, many people, in Great Britain and France especially, thought colonies were a good thing. They viewed their colonies as important markets for their manufactured goods and as suppliers of cheap **raw materials** for their industries. They also saw their own countries as being superior and therefore entitled to rule over the less-developed Asian or African nations.

Declining powers

Britain and France had entered the 20th century as two of the strongest nations in the world. Much of their wealth and prosperity came from their large **empires.** But the huge cost of World War I had drained this wealth, and by the 1920s and 1930s their empires were costing more to maintain than they were providing in resources.

Britain had lost most of Ireland in 1922, and the Dominions (Canada, Australia, New Zealand, and South Africa), although already self-governing, became fully independent in 1926. **Nationalist** groups that wanted independence for their own countries were especially powerful in British possessions such as India, Egypt, Iraq, and Persia (now Iran). France, too, was constantly struggling against nationalist groups in Indochina (now Vietnam, Laos, and Cambodia) and in French possessions in the Middle East and North Africa.

Gerrit Beneker's painting of an American construction worker in front of a towering line of skyscrapers symbolizes the optimism and prosperity of postwar America.

Up and coming powers

But as Britain and France struggled in the postwar world, other nations grew stronger. Even before World War I, the United States was the richest, most powerful country in the world.

The United States emerged from the war even stronger. If anyone was capable of challenging the French and British as "world leaders," it was the United States. But many Americans had not wanted to fight in the war in the first place. Many Americans also did not like the idea of empires and were not particularly happy that their country had helped Britain and France keep their colonies. Most historians agree that a spirit of **isolationism** seemed to dominate the United States throughout the 1920s and 1930s.

The **Soviet Union** was another huge country with great potential and a huge population. Until 1917, it was a nation ruled by a monarchy, or a system of government in which one person reigns over a kingdom or empire. Although some industrialization had taken place, the majority of its people still made a living off the land. Many people were **illiterate,** and poverty was widespread in both the cities and the rural areas. A **communist revolution** in 1917 overthrew the old **regime,** and the next twenty years were spent trying to turn the country into a modern, industrial power. The new regime was also occupied in establishing the authority of the communist government. In the process, **civil war,** famine, and huge **purges** left millions of people dead or imprisoned. Due to this turmoil, the Soviet Union was to play only a minor role in world affairs until 1939.

These Russian peasants, photographed in 1921, are victims of a famine brought about by the upheaval of a civil war. The war in Russia followed the 1917 communist revolution.

But other countries such as Germany, Italy, and Japan were ambitious. In the two decades following World War I, each would be taken over by **regimes** whose leaders were determined to make their nations rich and powerful. The aggressive way in which these governments pursued this policy was, as we shall see, one of the main causes of World War II.

Neville Chamberlain on the British Empire

"We are a very rich and vulnerable Empire, and there are plenty of poor adventurers not very far away who look upon us with hungry eyes."
Neville Chamberlain, British prime minister from 1937–40

Germany in the 1920s

Germany emerged from World War I as a new **democracy.** Its new government was called the Weimar **Republic** and was named after the German town in which the **constitution** was written. It was Germany's first democracy without a monarchy, and it came at a time of national humiliation and economic turmoil. The leaders who replaced Germany's military chiefs and monarch were inexperienced politicians. These men, rather than the military generals, were often blamed for the outcome of the Treaty of Versailles. They were also blamed for Germany's economic problems in the 1920s. Extremists such as Hitler found plenty of reasons for blaming Germany's troubles on "democracy."

Hard times

Fate had handed Germany's new democratic government a dreadful set of circumstances. The European victors were determined to make Germany pay for the cost of the war. A popular saying at the time said that Germany should be squeezed like a lemon until they didn't have anything left to pay. The European victors also wanted to ensure that Germany would remain too weak in the future to be able to fight in another conflict. These were harsh and unrealistic hopes, and they caused great hardship in Germany in the 1920s. The problem was obvious. Germany was being forced to pay high reparation payments, yet the country's economy was in financial tatters.

When Germany was unable to meet reparation payments in 1923, France and Belgium sent troops into Germany's industrial Ruhr region to take coal in place of the money owed. This was one occasion when the vast majority of the German people united behind their Weimar government in protest. Humiliations such as this fanned German hatred for its old enemies. After the occupation of the Ruhr, inflation became a huge problem. The value of money fell so dramatically that many businesses failed and there was mass **unemployment.**

*When Germany failed to make **reparation** payments in 1923, the French sent their army into the Ruhr, Germany's main industrial region. These French soldiers are cycling into the city of Essen, Germany.*

Gradual recovery

By the mid-1920s, Germany and the rest of Europe had begun to recover. The German economy revived, and the country settled into a brief four-year period of prosperity. In 1928 the German economy was almost as strong as it had been in 1914, and by the end of the 1920s, Germany was the second-largest exporter of goods in the world, after the United States.

Much of this recovery was the result of two economic packages put together by American **financiers** to make it easier for Germany to pay its **reparations.** The first, the Dawes Plan, was put into practice in 1924. It was named after Charles G. Dawes, an American businessman and diplomat who became U.S. vice president in 1925. While this plan did not reduce the amount of debt, it did help Germany by making the schedule of payments easier. But the plan proved to be unworkable. It was replaced in 1929 by the Young Plan, named after American businessman Owen D. Young. In this plan, total reparation payments were reduced by 75 percent and were to be paid in 59 annual installments. This would have taken the payments up to 1988. The first of these payments was made in 1930, but by 1931, Germany was once again in economic turmoil. The effects of a worldwide economic **depression** had made themselves felt, and Germany could not afford to pay. When Hitler came to power in 1933, he canceled all subsequent payments.

As Germany's economy collapsed, money lost its value. These German children are playing with worthless German bank notes.

Inflation

This is an economic term that describes a situation in which prices for goods go up dramatically and the value of money goes down. Wages buy increasingly less than they used to, and savings become less and less valuable. In Germany in the fall of 1923, inflation was so bad that prices in restaurants were put on blackboards so they could be changed frequently.

The Effects of the Great Depression

In the years after World War I, the United States had become increasingly prosperous. In 1929, however, the country's economy failed disastrously, triggered by the **stock market** crash on Wall Street in New York City. The stock market started to fail on October 24, a day now known as Black Thursday, and the crash climaxed on the following Tuesday. This led to severe and prolonged economic hardship all over the world, an era known as the Great **Depression.** In the 1920s, the stock market had gone through a period of massive growth when millions of people had invested in stocks and **shares** hoping to make quick and easy money. But when stock prices began to fall in late 1929, people in the United States panicked and hurriedly sold off their huge numbers of stocks and shares. This had a disastrous effect on the U.S. economy during the 1930s. People's savings disappeared and businesses ran out of money.

An American investor who has lost his entire savings in the stock market crash tries to make money by selling his car.

The United States suffered greatly, especially in the rural agricultural states. Concern for its own problems led many in the United States to turn away from world affairs, often against the wishes of the president at the time, Franklin D. Roosevelt, who was president from 1933 until 1945. Roosevelt was in a particularly difficult position. To help with economic recovery, he had set up a policy called "The New Deal," which called for the government to take an active role in creating work and encouraging business. In order to carry through these policies, he had to depend on support from politicians who were strongly in favor of **isolationism,** which meant keeping the United States away from any involvement in foreign affairs.

Global impact

The Great Depression had far-reaching global effects because so many different countries were dependent on the wealth of the United States. American factories bought **raw materials** from other countries, and American consumers bought goods that were imported from abroad. In addition, huge sums of money were lent by U.S. banks to countries trying to rebuild their war-shattered economies. During the depression, however, demand for goods suddenly dropped and bank loans were withdrawn. As a result,

The Great Depression

> "The Depression cast a pall [dark cloud] over the world. It was the worst peacetime catastrophe to afflict humanity since the Black Death [a plague in the 14th century]."
>
> Historian Piers Brendon in his book *The Dark Valley*

unemployment and bankruptcy, which is a state of financial ruin, rose throughout the world. Countries that had struggled to regain their prosperity after the war now found their economies failing once again.

With trade among nations so badly affected, **protectionism** flourished. In Great Britain, for example, from 1932 on, there was a tendency to trade with the countries of the **empire,** a policy known as "Imperial Preference." Increased economic competition turned into rivalry. This led led to growing hostility among nations.

Extreme solutions

All over the world, as wages fell, unemployment and desperate poverty rose. In the 1920s and 1930s, governments provided very little financial aid to help the poor and the unemployed. It is hardly surprising that in such difficult times many people turned to political extremes for a solution. These people believed that extreme measures were needed to combat the problems caused by the Great Depression.

In Germany and Japan, which were both severely hit by the Great Depression, **radical,** strongly **nationalistic** political groups gained power. Germany lacked oil and Japan had few **natural resources.** Because they needed these to supply their industries, the temptation grew stronger to take over other countries that did have natural resources.

*Unemployed German workers line up for state aid during the Great Depression of the early 1930s. Hitler offered men like these the prospect of work and prosperity while at the same time providing clear scapegoats for their troubles, such as **communists** and Jews.*

Mussolini and Fascist Italy

The years between the world wars produced some of the most brutal and cruel **dictators** of modern history, including Joseph Stalin in the **Soviet Union,** Adolf Hitler in Germany, General Francisco Franco in Spain, and Benito Mussolini in Italy. A dictator is a person who rules a country with total authority, often in a way that causes suffering.

Italy emerged as one of the victorious countries after World War I, but the country had failed to win the territory it wanted at the end of the war. After the war, Italy was overwhelmed by **strikes** and street fighting among rival political extremists, and its weak, **democratic** government collapsed.

In the early 1920s, Mussolini rose to power in Italian politics as leader of a **nationalistic, authoritarian** party called the **fascists.** A former **socialist,** he described himself as "an adventurer for all roads." This suited his party well, because it was made up of an odd mixture of people, including extremists, **trade unionists, anarchists,** and **republicans.**

Mussolini, in the official fascist uniform, makes an impassioned speech at an Italian rally in 1934. Like Hitler, he was an impressive public speaker.

The fascists come to power

In 1922, Mussolini announced that his followers would march on Rome, Italy, to seize control of the country and save it from lawlessness. Much to everyone's surprise, the Italian King Victor Emmanuel III took this as a cue to invite Mussolini to form a government. The king did this to avoid a **civil war** or a **communist revolution** similar to the one that had toppled the Russian monarchy in 1917. In 1925 Mussolini turned his rule into a **dictatorship.**

Despite Mussolini's often brutal treatment of political opponents, his party was widely popular, and Italy seemed to flourish under fascism. Strikes ended, industries produced more goods, and things seemed to run smoothly. It was often said at the time that "the trains ran on time." Drastic and dramatic reforms were announced. There would be "battles" for more land, more grain, more roads, and even for a higher birthrate.

Benito Mussolini (1883–1945)

Compared with other dictators Mussolini seems almost likeable, and it is easy to forget that he ordered opponents to be murdered. Like Hitler, this one-time teacher and journalist owed his success to his great skill as an orator, or speech maker. To many people in Italy at this time, he seemed like an inspired savior of his country. Known to Italians as "Il Duce" (pronounced Eel Doo-chey), or "the leader," he once described his policies as "97 cents worth of mere public clamor [shouting] and three cents worth of solid achievement."

Partners in crime: the Italian magazine Il Mattino Illustrato *celebrates a visit to Italy by Hitler in 1938 with this cover image of the German dictator standing beside Mussolini.*

However, Mussolini's rule lacked any real substance, and his reforms were weakened because of the widespread **corruption** that arose as fascist **cronies** seized control of local and national government organizations. As his policies failed at home in Italy, Mussolini increasingly looked to adventures abroad to build up support for his **regime.**

Mussolini and Hitler

Mussolini and German **Nazi** leader Adolf Hitler were fated to be political partners. Their political beliefs were very similar. Both men sought glory and power for their countries through authoritarian government and military conquest. Both dictators would die at the end of the war. However, when Hitler first came to power, Mussolini regarded him as a rival and actively disliked him, once referring to him as a "mad little clown." Hitler, however, admired the Italian leader greatly and modeled the Nazis on Mussolini's Fascist Party. For example, the Italian fascists had their own private army of violent ex-soldiers, known as blackshirts. Hitler copied this idea with his own brownshirts. Hitler also adopted other fascist ideas, such as Mussolini's **cult of personality,** his fascist youth organizations, and the fascist salute, which Italians were encouraged to make instead of a handshake because it was "more **hygienic.**"

Japan After World War I

During the 19th century, people in the **West** were used to thinking of the nations of East Asia as places to trade with or to conquer. Japan was an uncommon exception. Japan opened its ports to Western trade only when United States Navy commander Matthew Perry arrived with steamship gunboats in 1853. A close-knit, traditional society, Japan soon made use of Western technology, and within half a century it had become a modern, industrial nation. Its victory over the Russians in the Russo-Japanese war of 1904–1905 announced to the world that it was a confident, strong nation, capable of humiliating one of Europe's largest military powers.

Failing friendships

Japan forged close trade and cultural links with both Great Britain and the United States and had fought on the side of the **Allies** in World War I. But after the war, Japan was not treated as the great power it thought itself to be. At Versailles, the Japanese **delegates** were particularly angry when their European allies were not prepared to recognize the concept of racial equality and seemed to regard Japan as an inferior country. Then, in 1922, the Washington Naval Conference attempted to limit the size of Japan's navy. Japan was humiliated when it was agreed that its navy should be kept smaller than the navies of Britain or the United States. Like many other aspects of their **diplomacy** after World War I, the Allies had made a serious misjudgment. Their arrogant behavior played a part in turning Japan from a friendly nation into a fearful enemy.

Japan already had its own mini-**empire** and had been in control of Korea since 1905. Even after the Washington Naval Conference, Japan had a strong navy. It also had a powerful army led by generals who wanted to see Japan use its military strength to extend Japanese influence in Asia and to protect Japan "from **socialism.**" After World War I, Japan emerged as the major economic power in eastern and south Asia, but the 1920s and 1930s were to bring difficult times. Japan's prosperity was temporarily disrupted by the 1923 Tokyo earthquake, which flattened the city and left more than 140,000 dead. The worldwide **depression** also affected Japan very badly.

Turn to the right

Inside Japan, there was a noticeable shift in political thinking, which was partly due to this economic turmoil. Though Japan had made some progress toward establishing a **democracy,** it was still a very **conservative** society. In particular, Japan's military leaders, who had increasingly come to control the country during the 1930s, thought Japan should assert its power and authority over weaker neighboring countries. These military leaders were also more sympathetic to the **authoritarian** and militaristic ideals of the **fascist** countries of Germany and Italy.

Japan was a powerful industrial nation, but it had few **natural resources** of its own. During the early 1930s, Japan began to suffer from the effects of the depression. The silk industry was badly affected, and there was widespread poverty in both cities and rural areas of Japan. Japan's military leaders, thinking that the government was incapable of solving these problems, were preparing to act. They looked toward China and the East Asian **colonies** of the European powers such as Britain, France, and the Netherlands, which were also struggling with the depression. In colonies such as the Dutch East Indies, Indochina, Malaya, and other territories, there were resources such as oil and rubber, which they believed would bring prosperity to Japan.

This ominous poster from 1937 shows a Japanese boy dressed as a soldier armed with a bayonet and rifle. The poster points the way to Japan's future ambitions in the Asian Pacific.

Japan's military leaders

Many of Japan's politicians were disturbed by the growing influence of the country's military leaders. Koki Hirota, who was prime minister from 1936–37, said: *"The Military are like an untamed horse left to run wild. If you try head-on to stop it, you'll get kicked to death."*

The Rise of Hitler

The years after World War I were very difficult for Germany, but worse was to come. In this troubled atmosphere, a particularly gifted politician named Adolf Hitler managed to persuade the German people that only by his strong leadership would Germany's former power and prosperity be restored.

Hitler had first sprung to national attention in the 1920s. After World War I, this obscure Austrian corporal had been employed by the army to spy on extremist political organizations. As an undercover agent, he was sent to Munich, Germany, to join a **right-wing nationalist** group called the German Workers' Party. He ended up liking the party so much that he stayed in the group, and within a couple of years he became its president.

The Nazi Party

Hitler gave the group a new name—the National **Socialist** German Workers' Party, which soon became known as the **Nazi** Party. The Nazi Party called for all German people to be united into one nation. The party blamed the Jews and the **communists** for Germany's problems and vowed to avenge Germany for the humiliation of the Treaty of Versailles. The Nazis had a distinct identity, with colorful banners and a **swastika** symbol.

Inspired by Mussolini's "March on Rome," the Nazi Party led by Hitler intended to overthrow the Weimar government in a similar way. In November 1923, at a time of mass **unemployment, strikes,** and street fighting between rival political groups, Hitler and a group of armed Nazi thugs burst into a government meeting in a Munich beer hall. This action became known as the Beer Hall Putsch. At the beer hall, they announced they were going to set up a national government. But police fired on the Nazis as they marched toward the Bavarian War Ministry, and Hitler was arrested and sent to prison for eight months. After this, he decided that the way to power was through the conventional route of winning an election. But as Germany began to recover from the war and the country's economy prospered, Nazi support slumped dramatically.

Hitler salutes his supporters during a Nazi rally in 1927. Ceremonies such as this raised the profile of the Nazis and served to intimidate their political enemies.

Hitler's comeback

The Great **Depression** brought Hitler to power. In 1928 the Nazi vote was a mere 800,000, or 2.6 percent of the population of Germany. Yet by July of 1932, when the effects of the depression were being felt, it had risen to 13,750,000, or 37.3 percent. Hitler's Nazi Party appealed to many sections of German society. Powerful business people and industrialists thought Hitler would protect their country from a communist **revolution,** and they made generous donations to his party. Ordinary Germans, who at that time were often unemployed, began to feel that Hitler was the only politician capable of leading their country out of economic ruin. Like Mussolini, Hitler was also a hypnotically powerful speaker, and soon thousands, then millions, of Germans fell under his spell.

By January 1933, the Nazis held the greatest number of seats in the Reichstag, the German parliament, but they did not have a majority. A partnership with Chancellor Franz von Papen's Catholic Center Party brought them to power. Once in office, they swiftly ditched their political **allies** and took total control of Germany.

Once in power, Nazi hatred of the Jews became official state policy. Here, in April 1933, Nazi officials in Berlin place a notice on the window of a Jewish clothing shop, urging their fellow Germans not to shop there.

Mein Kampf

Hitler presented his philosophy in a book entitled *Mein Kampf* (My Struggle), which was published in 1925. Here are some of its main points:

- Hitler would lead the Aryan race (broadly meaning people of "pure" German blood) in a war to enslave the Slavs of eastern Europe and Russia, whom he considered inferior.
- The land they conquered would become *Lebensraum* ("living space") for the German people.
- The communist **Soviet Union** was Germany's greatest enemy and must be destroyed.
- The Jews were the greatest enemy of mankind and were to be "eliminated."

21

Hitler's Germany

Once in power, Hitler began to transform Germany, turning his extreme ideas into a living reality with remarkable speed. All aspects of daily life were put under the control of the **Nazi** Party. Everything from newspapers and radio broadcasts to schools and universities were controlled by the Nazis. The German people were bombarded with Nazi **propaganda** from every angle. Schoolchildren, for example, said prayers of thanks to Hitler rather than God and were encouraged to play "Jews and Aryans" rather than "Cowboys and Indians." Those who were brave enough to oppose the new **regime** faced the prospect of arrest by the feared *Gestapo* (the Nazi secret police) and execution or imprisonment in brutal **concentration camps.** The first of the permanent concentration camps was set up in Germany in 1933, soon after Hitler came to power.

A Nazi rally in Nuremberg in 1933. Rallies were seen to be a way of uniting the German people behind the Nazi cause.

Germany rearms

Unemployment had been one of Germany's greatest problems during the early years of the 1930s, so one of the Nazis' first tasks was to put the German people back to work. They did this by commissioning a series of public works—most notably Germany's *autobahn,* or highway, system. Schemes like this one put millions of people in Germany back to work, and by 1939, unemployment in Germany had been virtually eliminated.

Like almost everything else the Nazis did, however, the highway construction had a hidden purpose: it made the movement of troops and military equipment through Germany much easier. In 1933 Hitler told his chief ministers, "The next five years must be dedicated to the rearmament of the German people. Every publicly supported work-creation scheme must be judged from this standpoint: Is it necessary for the restoration of the military strength of the German people?" Over five years, government arms spending increased by 70 percent. Much of Germany's workforce had been put back to work to produce tanks, battleships, submarines, and warplanes.

Preparing the people for war

Hitler boasted that his regime, which was known as "The Third Reich," would last for a thousand years. To prepare for the wars that were intended to turn Germany into a global power, German children had to be prepared for the struggle to come. In 1936 a law was passed proclaiming that the "future of the German people depends on its youth. The entire German youth must therefore be prepared for its future duties." All German children had to join an organization called the Hitler Youth, for boys, and for girls, the League of German Maidens. Here their minds were further stoked with Nazi ideas about the superiority of the German race and the evils of **communism** and the Jews.

The Hitler Youth concentrated on developing physical fitness and military skills to prepare boys for life as soldiers. In the League of German Maidens, girls were taught that their greatest role in life was to have as many children as possible to provide Hitler with soldiers for his army.

These German girls are members of the League of German Maidens. Hitler had a low opinion of women and saw them mainly as providers of soldiers for his armies. By turning children into good Nazis, Hitler hoped to increase his power.

Adolf Hitler (1889–1945)

The son of a customs official, Hitler was born in Austria and grew up wanting to be an artist. His beliefs about the German "master race" and his hatred of the Jews were shared by many in the Austrian capital of Vienna, where Hitler lived as a homeless drifter before World War I. During the war, Hitler served as a corporal on the Western Front. He loved army life and was twice awarded the Iron Cross medal for bravery. The defeat of Germany in the war and the Versailles peace treaty that followed it filled Hitler with a lasting hatred for Germany's enemies and the "traitors" in the German government who he felt had betrayed Germany.

The Soviet Union Between the Wars

Of all the great powers involved in World War I, Russia suffered the most. Russia's ill-equipped troops fought many long and disastrous campaigns that left more than half the country's fighting forces dead or injured. By 1917, the huge Russian **empire** had collapsed into anarchy, the monarchy was toppled, and within a few months the **Bolshevik** Party, led by Vladimir Ilyich Lenin, seized power.

In 1918, Russia's **communist** leaders signed a humiliating peace treaty with Germany at the Russian city of Brest-Litovsk. The terms of the treaty dictated that Russia give up large amounts of territory on both its western and southern borders. This was followed by a bitter **civil war** between the new government of Russia and anticommunist forces aided by troops from Great Britain, France, and the United States. The war and the famine that accompanied the war claimed the lives of millions of Russians. It ended in victory for the communist government, and the country was renamed the USSR (Union of Soviet **Socialist Republics**). It was also known as the **Soviet Union.**

Lenin and the other leaders of the Soviet Union had hoped that further communist revolutions would sweep through all of Europe. When this failed to happen, they turned their efforts to strengthening the world's first communist nation.

Dictator Joseph Stalin (with his hand inside his coat) with fellow leaders of the Soviet Union in 1929. Within a decade almost all these men would fall victim to Stalin's infamous purges.

Stalin takes control

By January 1924, Lenin was dead. After a power struggle, the control of this huge nation finally passed to Joseph Stalin in 1928. More suffering was brought upon the Russian people as sweeping agricultural and industrial reforms were carried out. Millions died in further famines and in terrifying **purges,** in which persons suspected of being enemies of communism were executed or sent to labor camps. These places in which people were often worked to death were located in the desolate northern region of Siberia in eastern Russia.

In the 1930s, Stalin watched the rise of Hitler in Germany with alarm. The **Nazis** were sworn enemies of communism. Japanese intentions on Russia's southeastern border were another anxiety. Yet Stalin weakened his position even further when a devastating purge of the Russian military was carried out during 1937–38. This resulted in almost the entire senior officer corps being replaced by inexperienced but loyal communists and further weakened the strength of Soviet defenses.

Looking for friends

The Soviet Union searched for **allies** against the Nazis, but their **regime** was distrusted by almost every government in the world. Leading British politician Winston Churchill, for example, had referred to the Soviet Union as a "sullen, sinister Bolshevik state." **Western** nations were unwilling to commit to an **alliance** with the communist regime. So the Soviet Union entered the late 1930s with its army in utter disorder and with Nazi Germany threatening its western frontier. The Russian people had already endured twenty years of terror and hardship, and now even greater calamity awaited them. Before that happened, however, the world situation would change again. Two sworn enemies bizarrely became allies.

Supervised by the government's Red Army soldiers, thousands of Soviet workers walk through Moscow's central Red Square during the 1929 May Day rally celebrating the communist revolution.

Joseph Stalin (1879–1953)

Russia's leader from 1928, Stalin was one of the most cruel and feared **dictators** in history. Using the Soviet secret police to enforce his rule, his attempts to modernize Soviet Russia brought massive hardship to his people. Yet Stalin was also adored by many Russians, mainly because Soviet **propaganda** portrayed him as a godlike ruler but also because his ruthless leadership, at least in part, helped to save the Russian people from being conquered and enslaved by the Nazis. His character is tellingly illustrated by a remark he made in 1935 to a helper concerned at the Pope's reaction to the ill treatment of Catholics in the Soviet Union. "The Pope?" spluttered Stalin, asking about the Catholic leader's military strength, "How many divisions has he got?"

Franco and Spain

In 1936, a **left-wing** popular front coalition, or mixture of political parties, came to power in Spain, one of the most **conservative** Catholic countries in Europe. The popular front drew its support from mainly working-class voters and a diverse collection of Spanish **radicals, including republicans, socialists, communists,** and even **anarchists.** Such a government was too much to bear for Spain's deeply conservative army, which rebelled against its new leaders. The army rebels came to be under the leadership of General Francisco Franco. They were supported by the Catholic Church, most of the country's middle class, and Spain's **fascist** party, the Falangists. The resulting **civil war,** which was to last until 1939, became a battleground between the two political extremes of communism and fascism. The government's side became known as the Republicans, and General Franco's rebels were known as the **Nationalists.**

*Spain's **right-wing** leader General Franco is carried on the shoulders of some of his Nationalist soldiers in 1937. Within two years, his Nationalist troops had overwhelmed the Republican opposition.*

Hitler and Mussolini aid Franco

Franco's anticommunist sympathies meant he had much in common with Hitler and Mussolini, and both Germany and Italy lent him their support. Hitler sent tanks, aircraft, and about 10,000 men to drive, fly, and maintain these war machines. Germany's aircraft, the so-called Condor Legion of 100 planes, were especially effective and greatly superior to the air force of the Republicans. They guaranteed the Nationalists control of the skies, making it easier for their armies to advance without fear of attack from above. Not to be outdone, Mussolini sent 50,000 troops from the Italian army to help the Nationalists.

The Republicans had no help at all from the governments of their fellow **democracies** in **Western** Europe. Instead, they had to settle for the 40,000 volunteers from Europe and the United States who joined the International Brigades. The brigades were made up of people with left-wing ideas and of opponents of fascism. The Republicans, though, did receive help from the **Soviet Union,** who sent tanks and aircraft. The war lasted two years, and eventually Franco's better-equipped and better-organized Nationalists swept the Republicans from power. Altogether, about one million people died in the conflict.

Taking sides

Italy, Germany, and the Soviet Union had involved themselves in the Spanish civil war in the hope of winning an **ally** in southwest Europe. But after his victory, Franco was to prove a disappointment to the fascist **dictators.** Although he offered them goodwill, he cleverly kept his country out of World War II. As a result, Spain was able to avoid further devastation, and Franco was also able to ensure that his country would remain a fascist **dictatorship** until his death in 1975.

This photograph shows the ruined city of Guernica after heavy bombing by German warplanes. Bombing of civilian targets during the Spanish civil war caused great uneasiness in European cities.

Guernica

One of Hitler's motives for sending military help to the Nationalists in Spain was to give his army and air force firsthand experience of war. The German air force especially found the war an ideal training ground for their pilots. In 1937, the air force carried out one of the most infamous attacks of the conflict when the Basque capital of Guernica was bombed severely with heavy loss of civilian life. The bombing shocked the world, both in its demonstration of fascist ruthlessness and as an example of the terrible destruction that aircraft could bring to cities and their inhabitants. The effectiveness of the bombing of civilian targets caused great anxiety among Western Europe's city dwellers and also strengthened support for the British and French policy of trying to avoid war at all costs.

Japan's Ambitions for an Empire

Japanese soldiers march into the Chinese province of Manchuria. The barbaric behavior of troops like these toward China's civilian population caused widespread disgust throughout the world.

In the 1930s, Japan began to take giant strides in its quest to become the great power of the Asian Pacific. Across the Sea of Japan on the Asian mainland was the Chinese province of Manchuria. Japan had long regarded China as a natural **sphere of influence,** but Japan had to compete with other powers, notably Great Britain and the United States, who also saw China as a market for their goods. The **Soviet Union,** too, was wary of Japan's ambitions in China—it shared a common border with China. The Soviets did not want a hostile Japanese army looking to expand its empire on the doorstep of the Soviet Union.

In the 1920s and 1930s, China was in a state of political chaos. Rival warlords, or local military commanders, **communist** rebels, and the government of Jiang Jie-shi (also spelled Chiang Kai-shek) all competed for control of this huge country. Japan's increasingly aggressive military leaders decided conditions were perfect for a takeover. So, in 1931, Japanese troops poured into Manchuria in northern China. After a short campaign, they conquered the region. The territory, which was renamed Manchukuo, would stay in Japanese hands until the end of World War II.

It was a well-calculated risk. The Soviet Union, wrapped up in its own internal problems, did nothing. The League of Nations protested, but without an army and the full support of member countries, there was little else it could do. Britain and the United States were angry, but split over who should confront Japan.

Japan grows bolder

In 1934, the Japanese government formulated the Amau doctrine, which officially declared that China was within Japan's sphere of influence. In 1936, an army revolt in Japan put the military firmly in charge of the government, and Japan grew bolder still. In 1937, Japan launched an attack into China that became an all-out war. At first Japanese armies met with great success. In January 1938, Jiang Jie-shi's capital city of Nanjing, China, fell to the

Japanese. The world would later learn how the Japanese Imperial Army had laid waste to the city. Soldiers raped, looted, and murdered the city's inhabitants, killing more than 100,000 people. The massacre was carefully calculated to frighten Japan's neighbors so they would not be tempted to resist any future attack.

Further conquests

Japan was now set on a course to confront the older **colonial** powers of Britain, France, and the Netherlands in Asia. Japan's leaders correctly guessed, however, that their main rival for domination of the Asian Pacific was actually the United States. The European powers had their own problems to deal with, and their colonies would be easy to overcome. The United States would be more difficult to defeat.

By 1937 the war in East Asia had spread into the rest of China. These Japanese armored cars are driving through the streets of Shanghai, China.

Japan's claim to be master of Asia

Japan had many pressing reasons for wanting to expand its territory and influence in Pacific Asia. It was a small and already overcrowded country with a rapidly growing population. Before World War I, both the United States and Australia had been popular destinations for Japanese people wishing to emigrate. By the 1930s, both of these countries refused to allow more Japanese people to settle there. Although Japan had a powerful industrial base, it had few **natural resources.** Japan's leaders felt they had as much right as any other country to become a colonial power, and from 1940 on they promoted this policy with the **propaganda** slogan "Asia for Asians." However, as a conquering colonial power, Japan was just as exploitative and often considerably crueler than the European powers it replaced.

Italy's New Roman Empire

Protected by his imperial guard, the Abyssinian Emperor Haile Selassie is pictured here shortly after his country was invaded by the Italian army in 1935.

International relations throughout the 1930s were dominated by aggressive **right-wing regimes** challenging the existing world order. Japan invaded China. Germany, as we shall see later in this book, challenged and overturned the borders imposed by the Treaty of Versailles. In Italy, Mussolini's domestic policies began to falter, so he turned to foreign adventures to distract the Italian people from the failures of his regime.

Adventures in Africa

Italy had a glorious imperial past. The Roman **Empire** had once ruled over most of the known world. Mussolini dreamed of creating a new Italian empire to rival the old. Italy had some **colonial** possessions in Africa, notably Libya, Eritrea, and Italian Somaliland, which shared a border with Abyssinia (now called Ethiopia). Abyssinia, a mountainous African kingdom, was one of the few independent nations left on the continent. Most of the rest of Africa had been colonized by other European powers. Abyssinia, Mussolini believed, would be a good place to start the creation of the new Roman Empire, especially because the country had close trading links with Italy.

The League of Nations

This international organization had been set up after World War I to solve disputes among nations by peaceful means. Its members were committed to open **diplomacy** and were bound by an understanding that they would abide by the League's decisions. As a final resort, League members could impose economic **sanctions** on any country whose actions they disapproved of. However, without support from the United States and with no military force of its own, the League was powerless against any determinedly aggressive nation. The actions of Italy, Japan, and Germany in the 1930s totally undermined the credibility of the League.

Mussolini thought that the poorly equipped Abyssinian army would be easy to defeat, and in October 1935 he attacked them with 300,000 troops armed with the advanced weapons of 20th-century warfare. Despite the poison gas and aerial bombardment they were subjected to, the barefoot soldiers of the Abyssinian Emperor Haile Selassie managed to hold off the Italians for a whole eight months before the capital city, Addis Ababa, fell to Italian forces in May 1936.

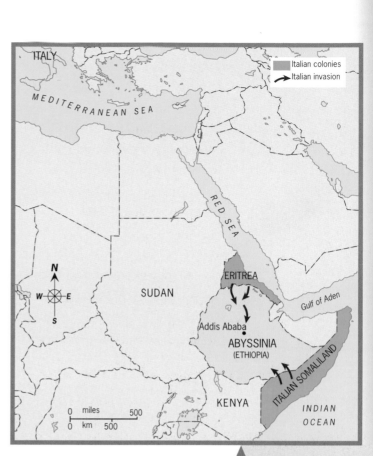

European reaction

The **Western** European powers reacted with dismay and the League of Nations protested, but no country was willing to act against Italy's aggression. Great Britain and France, especially, were determined not to drive Mussolini into a closer partnership with Hitler. Nevertheless, their reluctance to act resulted in Mussolini forging just such a partnership. In 1936, Germany and Italy announced that they had formed an "**Axis,**" or hub, around which, they grandly announced, "all European states can also assemble."

Mussolini's empire building began with the invasion of Abyssinia in 1935–36. By 1941, Italy was forced to give up its African colonies of Eritrea and Somaliland, and Abyssinian independence was restored.

A troubled partnership

History depicts Hitler and Mussolini as firm friends and close **allies.** But this was not always the case. When they first met in 1934, Mussolini described Hitler as a "barbarian." Italy objected fiercely to an early Nazi attempt to seize Austria in 1934 and initially saw Germany as a rival for influence in the Balkan region of southeastern Europe. When they did become close allies, Germany's friendship with Italy would do Hitler few favors.

Mussolini hoped to inspire his people to be more warlike with the slogan, "Better to be a lion for a day than a sheep for 100 years." But his real problem was that the Italian people had no appetite for war. It was his own desperate desire for glory that would bring Italy into World War II on the side of the **Nazis** and lead both himself and his country to destruction.

Hitler Tests the Water

If Hitler felt history had been cruel to Germany in 1918, then he could hardly complain in the 1930s. The decade was a perfect time for someone with his vision of Germany's future to push the boundaries and see what he could get away with. The United States was pursuing its policy of **isolationism.** The **Soviet Union** was preoccupied with establishing its own brand of **communism.** Great Britain and France were so keen to reach an understanding with Hitler that he must have thought they would let him get away with anything.

Germany was gathering **allies,** too. After initial hostility from Italy, Mussolini was drawing closer to the **Nazis.** The Japanese, seeing Nazi Germany as an enemy of the Soviet Union, joined an anticommunist agreement with Germany in 1936. Italy joined a year later. The agreement was called the Anti–Comintern Pact. All three powers had a desire to reorganize the world in a way that suited them better.

Soon after Hitler came to power in Germany in 1933, he set about rearming the nation. This picture shows a German airplane factory that made Heinkel bombers, which were later used to bomb European cities.

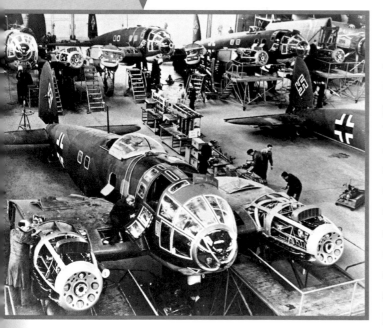

Plans for world domination

But while Japan and Italy just wanted to expand their **colonial** possessions, Germany had ambitions that were far greater. Hitler wanted his country to rule the world. He saw the achievement of this aim as a two-stage plan. In the first stage, Germany was to regain the territory lost at the Treaty of Versailles and also take over territory in Europe. When Germany controlled *mitteleuropa* (central and eastern Europe), it would have access to coal, iron ore, oil, and a workforce to build a war machine capable of taking Hitler's plan to stage two.

In stage two, he intended to build an **empire** to the east of Germany to provide *Lebensraum,* or living space, for his German master race. This, in effect, meant the conquest of Poland and European Russia. Once these territories had been incorporated, Germany would be the strongest power on Earth.

GERMANY PREPARES FOR WAR
THE FIGURES BELOW SHOW THE AMOUNT AND THE PROPORTION OF GERMANY'S NATIONAL INCOME THAT WAS SPENT ON ARMAMENTS FROM THE YEAR HITLER GAINED POWER TO THE YEAR WORLD WAR II BEGAN.

1933 2% (1.2 MILLION REICHSMARKS)
1936 11% (10.2 MILLION REICHSMARKS)
1939 30% (38 MILLION REICHSMARKS)

Step one and onward

Almost as soon as he gained power, Hitler started to rearm Germany. After World War I, as part of the Treaty of Versailles, an area of land known as the Saar (see map on page 9) was put under the control of the League of Nations. In 1935 this coal-rich region voted to return to Germany. Then, from 1936, Hitler began to carry through stage one of his master plan. In March of that year, German troops entered the demilitarized Rhineland—the common border with France. Protests against this violation of the Treaty of Versailles were made, but no direct action was taken by France or Britain. It was commonly said in Britain that Hitler was "only marching into his own backyard."

In March 1938, German troops entered Austria and the country was united with Germany. This was another move strictly forbidden by the treaty. Again no action was taken. Then Hitler turned his attention to another part of eastern Europe. This was the Sudetenland (see map on page 9) in Czechoslovakia, home to some three million German speakers. Certain that Germany would have to fight to regain this territory, Hitler's generals were instructed to prepare their armies for war. Meanwhile, France and Britain had been watching Germany's growing strength with increasing alarm, and they chose this moment to intervene.

Hitler makes a triumphant entry into Vienna, the capital city of Austria, following the country's union with Germany in March 1938.

Anschluss

The *Anschluss* was the name given to the unification of Germany and Austria. This event took place in March of 1938. Austria already had a strong Nazi movement of its own, and when Hitler sent his troops into Austria many people came out of their homes to welcome them.

Appeasement and Munich

In the years between World War I and World War II, Great Britain and France were two of the greatest powers in Europe. But by 1938, Germany had once again turned into a major rival. The **Nazis** were openly rearming and had demonstrated the effectiveness of their tanks and warplanes in the Spanish **civil war.** The Saar, the Rhineland, and Austria had all been fully incorporated into the Reich, or the German state. Now, Hitler had begun to demand the Sudetenland. This was land that was included as part of Czechoslovakia in 1917–1918, when that new country's borders were being drawn. Hitler had considerable support among the German-speaking Sudetenlanders, most of whom were happy to be united with Germany.

Ill-prepared

The British and French prime ministers, Neville Chamberlain and Edouard Daladier, were both faced with an awkward situation. Both of them wanted to protect their country's power and prestige. They also did not want to allow Hitler to boss them around. But both were compromised. Their armed forces were not ready for a war. Their people did not want a war, and the memory of the dreadful slaughter of World War I was still fresh in their minds. Additionally, British and French leaders both recognized that Germany had been badly treated by the Treaty of Versailles. They therefore felt that Germany had the right to correct this situation. Also, there was considerable support for **fascism** in France, and in Britain many upper-class people secretly admired Hitler. Both countries saw the Nazis and fascist Italy as potential **allies** against the **communist Soviet Union.**

Hitler could appear warm and charming when the occasion demanded. Here, he greets British Prime Minister Chamberlain with a friendly smile during one of their meetings at Munich in September 1938.

All these various strands came together in a policy known as **appeasement.** But appeasement assumed that Britain and France were allowing Hitler to redraw the map of Europe on terms that were acceptable to all three nations.

Hitler resented this attitude, but he was clever enough to take advantage of it. As his army prepared to invade Czechoslovakia to annex the Sudetenland, prime ministers Chamberlain and Daladier, supported by Mussolini, requested a meeting with Hitler. All four leaders met in

Munich, Germany, in September 1938, where it was agreed that the Sudetenland would be given to Germany. In return, Hitler promised this was "the last territorial claim I have to make in Europe."

Peace in our time

History has not been kind to Chamberlain and Daladier. They are remembered as gullible fools who were tricked by a cunning Hitler. Maybe they were tricked, but at the time their policy of appeasement was widely popular. Daladier was greeted by a crowd of half a million people when he returned to Paris. When Chamberlain returned to London clutching a signed agreement from Hitler and declaring "it is peace in our time," he was met with widespread jubilation.

Appeasement had some advantages. In practical terms, there was little Great Britain or France could do to help Czechoslovakia. Besides, by delaying war with Germany, Chamberlain gave the British more time to build up its armed forces. Later, this would be a vital factor in Germany's failure to defeat Britain when war finally came.

The German occupation of Prague in March 1939 caused great anger in the streets of the Czech capital, but little real resistance.

Appeasement in East Asia

The British government also applied the policy of appeasement to Japan. They recognized that Japan was a powerful nation that deserved some measure of influence over its neighboring countries in Asia. Japan's occupation of Manchuria was accepted, partly because the British thought a powerful Japan would prevent the Soviet Union from extending its communist influence into Asia. The fact that there was very little Britain could do about Japanese aggression also aided this acceptance.

Europeans who took the Munich agreement at face value slept soundly for a few more months. Then, in March 1939, Nazi soldiers marched into the rest of Czechoslovakia. Few people now doubted that war could be avoided. In the summer of 1939, Nazi Germany turned its attention to the nation of Poland. The people of the continent held their breath and waited for the spark that would ignite another war.

The Nazi-Soviet Pact

Throughout the 1930s, the **Soviet Union** had been regarded with fear and distrust by both the **Western democracies** and the **right–wing dictatorships** of Europe. However, as war loomed at the end of the decade, leaders on all sides considered the benefits of an **alliance** with the world's only **communist** nation.

A failed alliance

In March 1939, German soldiers marched into Prague and claimed the western half of Czechoslovakia as their own. The agreement Germany had made with Great Britain and France at Munich had obviously failed. A month later, the Soviet Union suggested an alliance with Britain and France against Germany. The proposal was met with only lukewarm interest. Britain hoped for support against Germany from other countries in eastern Europe, particularly Poland. Poland, in particular, feared that the Soviet Union wanted to win back land lost after World War I.

Talks among Great Britain, France, and the Soviet Union continued over the summer, but France and Britain deliberately delayed any final commitment. Britain, for example, sent only minor officials to the Soviet Union to negotiate. These officials had no real power to make decisions. They also traveled by boat, rather than plane, so they took weeks to get there. Eventually, Britain and France decided the Soviet Union was too unreliable and that they could do without its support. The talks ground to a halt in August 1939.

David Low's classic illustration of Hitler and Stalin greeting each other with cordial insults over the body of a dead Polish soldier. This cartoon captures the utter disbelief many people felt on hearing of the Nazi-Soviet Pact.

Germany steps in

Meanwhile, **Nazi** foreign minister Joachim von Ribbentrop had also approached his Soviet counterpart, Vyacheslav Molotov. When talks with the Western democracies failed, Molotov agreed to meet Ribbentrop. Ribbentrop knew the Nazis planned to invade Poland at any moment and therefore was particularly eager to make an agreement. Hitler sent a telegram to Stalin, who replied within two hours. Ribbentrop flew to Moscow in Russia, and in the early hours of

The Nazi-Soviet Pact

- The Nazis and Soviets would not attack each other.
- Russia would supply Germany with **raw materials** in return for weapons.
- Germany agreed that the Soviets should gain control of Finland, the Baltic States, and east Poland.
- The Soviets agreed that Germany should gain control of west Poland.

August 24, 1939, a treaty was agreed on in which both countries promised not to attack each other.

Many people were surprised and bewildered when they heard the news that the Nazis and Soviets had signed a nonaggression pact. After all, they were known to despise each other's political **regimes.** But the pact suited them both, at least for the time being. Hitler wanted to avoid a simultaneous war on Germany's east and west frontiers—a similar situation had considerably hindered the success of Germany in World War I. The Soviets, for their part, were unprepared for war. Their army was still recovering from the effects of Stalin's latest **purge.**

Nazi and Soviet troops have a friendly meeting in late September 1939, following each country's occupation of sections of Poland.

Europe is mine

When he heard news that the treaty had been agreed, Hitler gloated, "Now Europe is mine." Nothing, it seemed, could stop him from invading Poland, and with the Soviets' agreement, he was sure that France and Great Britain would not intervene. Referring to Chamberlain and Daladier he sneered, "They are little worms. I saw them in Munich. I'll cook them a stew they'll choke on." Orders for the long-imagined invasion of Poland were put into motion, and Germany's soldiers and tanks headed east to the border.

War Breaks Out

Germany's seizure of the rest of Czechoslovakia in March 1939 marked the end of **appeasement.** Hitler had humiliated Great Britain and France, and both countries were now determined not to allow that to happen again. Hitler failed to understand this. Instead, he thought that Poland was of no more significance to the **Western democracies** than Czechoslovakia. The 1938 Czechoslovakian crisis had, after all, been publicly described by British Prime Minister Chamberlain as "a quarrel in a faraway country between people of whom we know nothing."

Hitler failed to understand that France and Britain did not look on his invasion of Poland in isolation. Instead, Hitler's rivals saw the invasion as Germany going one step too far. France and Britain now felt they had little choice but to stop Germany from becoming too powerful in Europe. In 1939, the military balance among the three countries was about even—that is, their military forces were of similar strength. If Germany was allowed to take over Poland without a fight, Germany would become much stronger than its opponents. Besides, earlier in the year Britain and France had given Poland guarantees that they would attack Germany if Poland was invaded. In expectation of this, both France and Britain had begun preparing for war.

Ready to fight

By 1939, Britain especially was better prepared to fight than it had been at the time of the Munich agreement a year earlier. In April 1939, **conscription** was introduced to bring the armed forces up to wartime strength. New weapons were also now in service, especially fast monoplanes such as Hurricanes and Spitfires. Work was also under way on developing sophisticated radar technology that could spot approaching enemy aircraft hundreds of miles away.

So, when German troops poured over the Polish border, Britain and France both issued ultimatums, or final warnings, that called on Germany to withdraw. When these were ignored, Hitler found himself, on September 3, 1939, at war with the world's two greatest **empires.** Only later did Hitler realize how badly he had underestimated his enemies' will to fight. He had spent the last four years taking huge risks, but this time he had overreached himself.

This painting shows a squadron of Spitfires attacking German Heinkel bombers during the Battle of Britain in 1940. Germany's failure to defeat the Royal Air Force saved Britain from invasion.

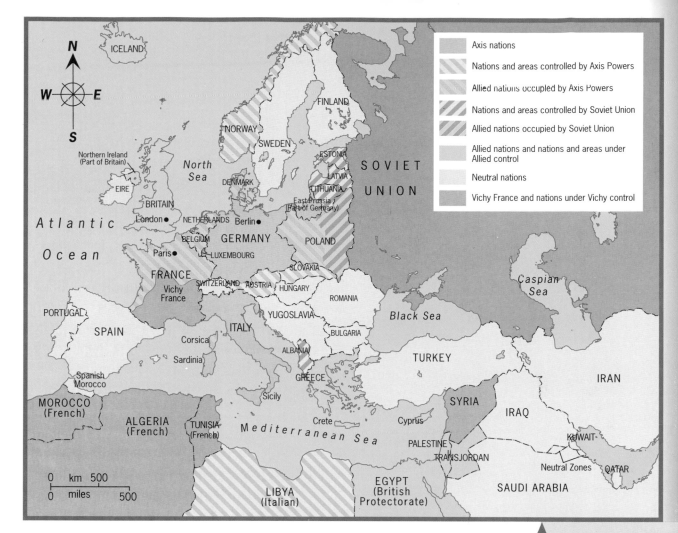

Europe in 1940. The **Axis** powers controlled much of Europe by this time. The Germans occupied northern France, while southern France was put under the control of a new government that supported the Axis powers. The following year, Hungary, Romania, and Bulgaria joined the Axis.

Nazi victories

At first, everything went Hitler's way. Poland crumbled before Germany's powerful army and its devastating *blitzkrieg* tactics. The following year, Hitler turned his attention north and west and quickly overran Denmark and Norway, Belgium, the Netherlands, and Luxembourg. By June of 1940, the German army occupied Paris. It was at this point that Mussolini brought Italy into the war, spreading the fighting to the eastern Mediterranean and North Africa. Only Britain lay undefeated in the west, and only because the channel provided a natural barrier that was difficult for armies to cross.

To carry off a successful invasion of Britain, Hitler had to win control of the skies. The Battle of Britain, fought by the Royal Air Force (RAF) against the **Nazi** *Luftwaffe* from July to September 1940, was Hitler's first defeat. In a close battle, Germany's warplanes were narrowly defeated by the RAF's more speedy and maneuverable Hurricanes and Spitfires. With the rest of Europe at his feet, Hitler turned instead to his next great project—the invasion of the **Soviet Union.** It would be his greatest mistake.

From European War to World War

Hitler had not originally planned to attack the **Soviet Union** before the middle of the 1940s, but by 1941 he had conquered large areas of mainland Europe. Germany's position was made even stronger by the Tripartite Pact, which had been signed by Germany, Italy, and Japan in September 1940. In the pact, the countries agreed to cooperate in their ambitions to establish "a new order" in Europe and Asia. Hungary, Romania, Slovakia, and Bulgaria joined them in the spring of 1941. After the fall of France, Hitler declared, "I shall go down in history as the greatest German of them all," and brought forward plans to invade the Soviet Union.

Despite his optimism, Hitler had some unresolved problems. Britain was

This picture shows Soviet troops pushing a piece of antitank artillery through a snowy field during the Battle of Moscow in 1941.

undefeated, and Hitler's **ally,** Mussolini, was proving to be a hindrance. Before the planned invasion of the Soviet Union could go ahead in the late spring of 1941, German troops had to be diverted to Africa, the Balkans, and Greece to help out Italian armies that were struggling. Toward the end of the war Hitler admitted, "It is in fact quite obvious that our Italian **alliance** has been of more service to our enemies than to ourselves." As a result, the invasion of the Soviet Union was postponed for a vital month, leaving the German armies with less time to overrun the Soviet Union before the fall rains slowed down the fighting and the harsh winter brought it to a standstill.

When the invasion (code named "Barbarossa") finally came on June 22, 1941, it was initially an astounding success. Hitler had predicted that the "rotten" Soviet **regime** would rapidly collapse. By the fall, advanced units of the German army were already at the gates of Moscow, the nation's capital city. But the Russians bravely fought back. Twenty million of its citizens—on average about 19,000 a day—would die defeating the **Nazis.** Hitler's dream of world conquest turned into a nightmare on the vast, open plains and mud and snow of Soviet Russia.

War in the Pacific

The invasion of the Soviet Union widened the war's scope, but it was the Japanese who turned World War II into a truly global conflict. Germany's **Axis** partner Japan took full advantage of the German conquest of France by occupying French Indochina (now Vietnam, Laos, and Cambodia) in 1940. Britain and the United States had already responded to Japan's aggressive military policies by imposing an embargo, or ban, on iron and oil exports destined for Japan. The need to seize new sources of these vital **raw materials** before their own stockpiles ran out led Japan's military leaders to decisive action.

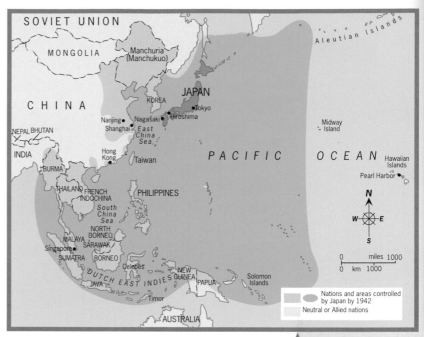

Japanese expansion in the Pacific, 1931–42.

Japan's most powerful rival in the Pacific was the United States, so a surprise attack on America's main military base in the Pacific, Pearl Harbor, Hawaii, was planned. Carried out with complete surprise on December 7, 1941, it was a stunning blow. While the United States reeled, Japan carried through an bold and immensely successful campaign, attacking both American and European possessions. By the middle of 1942, Japan's armies controlled the entire Asian Pacific rim, from the tip of the Aleutian Islands through to Hong Kong, the Philippines, Singapore, Burma, and down to Java and New Guinea.

The Pearl Harbor attack had other dramatic consequences. Hitler, drunk on his successes in Europe, declared war on the United States. Finally awakened out of **neutrality,** the United States declared war on Japan and then on Japan's allies in Europe. The United States turned its hugely powerful economy to winning the war. Within a couple of years, its factories would be producing one new warplane every five minutes. Against such military might, the forces of Germany and Japan didn't really stand a chance.

A gloomy future?

Admiral Yamamoto, the architect of the Pearl Harbor attack, responded to praise for its success with the prophetic words *"I fear we have only succeeded in awakening a sleeping tiger."*

Learning the Lessons

"I did so hope that we were going to escape these tragedies. But I sincerely believe that with that madman it was impossible." So wrote Neville Chamberlain about his struggle to restrain Hitler. Was World War II inevitable? The answer is probably yes. World War I had ended in a vengeful treaty that was dismissed by one French general as "a twenty year cease-fire." Most importantly, in some of the countries where economic hardship brought desperate times, especially during the Great **Depression, authoritarian regimes** were able to seize power. The worst of these regimes was led by Hitler. His agenda was to make Germany *the* global power, to destroy **communism** and the Jewish race, and to conquer land in eastern Europe. This could not fail to bring him into conflict with other nations. Mussolini's desire to create a new Italian **empire** and Japan's wish to dominate Pacific Asia brought conflict to North Africa, China, and much of Asia.

Certain of victory, the "Big Three," Stalin (left), Roosevelt (center), and Churchill (right) meet in February 1945 to decide the fate of the postwar world.

Looking back from the present, we might wonder if events would have turned out differently if the League of Nations had not been so weak, or if Great Britain and France had not adopted the policy of **appeasement,** or if the United States had turned away from **isolationism** earlier. Perhaps, then, it would not have taken a world war, and all the suffering that the war caused, to remove these **dictators** from power.

Consequences of the war

As the war progressed, the conquering armies of the **Axis** powers were pushed back to their home countries. Hitler committed suicide, and Mussolini was captured trying to flee Italy and shot. When the fighting stopped after two atomic bombs were dropped on Japan, 50 million people had been killed. Defeated France and exhausted Britain gradually came to realize they were no longer the major world powers they had once been. In the decades following the war, their empires slipped away from them.

The **Soviet Union** had fought the **Nazi** armies from Moscow back

through eastern Europe and all the way to Berlin. Stalin had seen his country twice attacked by the **West** in twenty years, and he was determined this should not happen again. Soviet soldiers stayed in East Germany and eastern Europe, and the Soviets set up communist regimes in all the nations between themselves and West Germany. These so-called "buffer states" were a barrier against further attacks. Only when the Soviet Union collapsed in 1991 were the countries of eastern Europe allowed to choose their own governments.

Determined that there should be "no more Pearl Harbors," the United States turned away from **isolationism** and maintained a military presence in Europe and throughout the world. Today, France, Britain, and Germany now strive for closer political ties within the European Union, and the thought of war among them is hard to imagine. Perhaps the most positive lesson learned from the war has been in the success of the United Nations, especially when compared with the failure of the League of Nations that preceded it.

The war in Europe comes to an end. A Russian soldier flies the Soviet flag from the Berlin Reichstag, or parliament building, on April 30, 1945.

The United Nations
The United Nations was set up in San Francisco in 1945. The principal of racial equality was written into its charter. Additionally, instead of relying only on economic **sanctions** to enforce its rulings, it was given military "teeth" in the form of fighting forces from its members. Over the last half century, the UN has been involved in major conflicts throughout the world, from the Middle East and the Balkans to former **colonial** territories in Africa. Its troops are stationed in trouble spots to play a peacekeeping role, keeping warring factions apart.

Timeline

1889	Birth of Adolf Hitler
1917	Lenin leads **Bolshevik revolution** in Russia
1918	March: Russia surrenders to Germany at the treaty of Brest-Litovsk
	November: World War I ends with Germany's armies in full retreat
1919	June: Treaty of Versailles
	September: Treaty of Germain-en-Laye with Austria
1920	Treaty of Trianon with Hungary
1921	Hitler becomes leader of the **Nazi** party
1922	Mussolini seizes power in Italy
1923	Nazi Beer Hall Putsch in Munich leads to arrest and imprisonment of Hitler
	Occupation of the Ruhr
1924	Dawes Plan restructures German **reparations**
1928	Stalin becomes leader of the **Soviet Union**
1929	Young Plan further reduces and restructures reparations
	September: **Stock market** crash leads to worldwide economic **depression**
1931	Japan invades Manchuria
1933	Hitler and Nazis come to power in Germany
1934	Hitler and Mussolini first meet
1935	Italy invades Abyssinia
1936	March: German troops move into the Rhineland
	July: Spanish **civil war** begins (ends 1939)
	October/November: Germany, Italy, and Japan declare themselves **Axis** powers
1937	Japan invades rest of China
1938	January: Nanjing falls to Japanese army and more than 100,000 are massacred
	March: Germany invades Austria and unites the two countries
	September: Munich agreement allows Germany to occupy Sudetenland in Czechoslovakia
1939	March: German army moves beyond the Sudetenland into Czechoslovakia
	August: Nazi-Soviet Pact
	September: Germany invades Poland
	Great Britain and France declare war on Germany
1941	June: Germany invades the Soviet Union
	December: Japan attacks Pearl Harbor and the United States joins World War II
	Germany declares war on the United States
1943	Italy surrenders
1945	Germany and Japan defeated
	United Nations founded

Further Reading

Chorlton, Windsor. *Weapons and Technology of World War II.* Chicago: Heinemann Library, 2002.

Downing, David. *Benito Mussolini.* Chicago: Heinemann Library, 2001.

Downing, David. *The Great Depression.* Chicago: Heinemann Library, 2001.

Downing, David. *Joseph Stalin.* Chicago: Heinemann Library, 2001.

Grant, R. G. *Armistice 1918.* New York: Raintree Steck-Vaughn, 2000.

Masters, Nancy. *Airplanes of World War II.* Minnetonka, Minn.: Capstone Press, 1998.

Reynoldson, Fiona. *Key Battles of World War II.* Chicago: Heinemann Library, 2001.

Sheehan, Sean. *Germany and Japan Attack.* New York: Raintree Steck-Vaughn, 2001.

Stone, Tanya Lee. *The Great Depression and World War II.* New York: Raintree Steck-Vaughn, 2001.

Tames, Richard. *Pearl Harbor: The U.S. Enters World War II.* Chicago: Heinemann Library, 2001.

Taylor, David. *Adolf Hitler.* Chicago: Heinemann Library, 2002.

Glossary

alliance agreement between countries that want to support one another

allies people, political parties, or countries working together. "Allies" refers to Great Britain and its empire, France and its empire, and U.S. forces in World War I and World War II.

anarchy condition in a country when there is no government or law and order. An anarchist is a person who believes in doing away with government.

appeasement policy of keeping an enemy from doing more harm by giving in to some of their demands

armistice agreement to stop fighting

authoritarian demanding strict obedience to government

Axis alliance of Germany, Japan, Italy, and other countries during World War II

Bolshevik name given to the communists who seized power in Russia in 1917

civil war war fought among people of the same country

colonies countries owned and controlled by another country

communist believer in communism, a political system in which the government controls the wealth and industry of a country

concentration camp prison camp in which prisoners are often treated very brutally

conscription required service in the armed forces

conservative preferring the preservation of established customs and traditions at the expense of new ideas

constitution political ideas and rules that determine how a state or country is run

corruption in politics, a state of affairs in which political decisions are decided by bribes and other favors, rather than any right or wrong considerations

cronies in politics, members of a party who owe their jobs in government to the fact that they have a personal friendship with senior members of that party

cult of personality deliberate creation of a godlike image of a political leader, characteristic of states or countries governed by a dictator

delegate person who represents an organization, region, or country at a conference

democracy rule of a country by a government elected by the people

depression in economic terms, a period in time when businesses do badly and many people are unemployed and poor

dictatorship political situation where one person has absolute power to rule a country

diplomacy conduct of relations between countries

empire collection of colonies

fascism political philosophy that glorifies power, military might, and nationalism and that is opposed to communism and democracy

financier person who invests large amounts of money that belong to someone or something else, such as a corporation or the government

ghetto poverty-stricken part of a city where people of the same race or nationality were sometimes forced to live

hygienic clean, healthy

illiterate unable to read or write

intelligentsia highly educated members of a society

isolationism in politics, the process of remaining free from alliances with other nations, or becoming involved with the affairs of other nations

left-wing in political terms, leaning toward a socialist or communist viewpoint

liquidate destroy

motorized troops troops that travel by some form of motorized transportation, as opposed to on foot

nationalist someone who wants his or her country to be independent of its colonial masters. This term can also refer to someone who unreasonably puts the interests of his or her country before all other countries.

natural resources naturally occurring materials such as coal or iron ore or foods to which a country has access

Nazi member of the National Socialist Party in Germany during Hitler's time. The philosophy of Nazism is basically the same as fascism.

neutral not being involved in conflict

propaganda misleading information that is used to try to persuade people to adopt a certain viewpoint

protectionism economic term broadly meaning buying goods made in your own territory and trying to prevent imports by imposing tariffs

purge term relating to the widespread killing or imprisonment of sections of Soviet society perceived by Joseph Stalin to be a threat to his communist regime

radical someone who supports extreme changes. A radical change is a big change.

raw material naturally occurring material such as iron ore or rubber that can be turned into manufactured products by industry

reconciliation settling of quarrels and resentments between former enemies

regime form of government that often rules by force

reparations after a war, money paid by a defeated nation to the nation or nations for the damage its actions, such as invasion or bombing, caused

republican someone who does not support a monarchy

revolution politically, a rebellion that leads to the overthrow of a government

right-wing in political terms, leaning toward a more conservative viewpoint. Fascists and Nazis are extreme right-wing political groups.

sanctions withholding of goods and raw materials exported to a country to express disapproval of that country's actions

share financial term for a document showing an investment in a company, ownership of which entitles a person to some of that company's profits

socialist someone who supports the political system whereby a country's wealth is shared equally and where some of the main industries are run by the government

Soviet Union another name for the Union of Socialist Soviet Republics (USSR), a communist country including Russia that collapsed in 1991

sphere of influence political term meaning an area of the world where one country feels it should be allowed to intervene

SS elite Nazi troops

stalemate situation in which neither side can win

stock market financial institution where shares are sold

strikes refusing to work as a way of making a protest

swastika cross with arms bent at right angles. The Nazis used the swastika as their symbol.

trade union organized group of workers set up to improve pay and working conditions

unemployment when people do not have jobs

West, Western political rather than geographical term for the rich industrialized countries of northern and western Europe, North America, Australia, and New Zealand

Index